D0871934

The KidHaven Science Library

Electricity

by Sheila Wyborny

KIDHAVEN
PRESS™

THOMSON
—————TM
GALE

San Diego • Detroit • New York • San Francisco • Cleveland
New Haven, Conn. • Waterville, Maine • London • Munich

For more information, contact
KidHaven Press
27500 Drake Rd.
Farmington Hills, MI 48331-3535
Or you can visit our Internet site at http://www.gale.com

LIBRARY OF CONGRESS CATALOGING-IN-PUBLICATION DATA

Wyborny, Sheila, 1950–
   Electricity : by Sheila Wyborny.
      p. cm. — (The Kidhaven science library)
   Summary: Explains some examples of electricity in nature, early experiments with electricity, the development of use of electric power, and possibilities for the future.
   Includes bibliographical references and index.
   ISBN 0-7377-1535-9 (hbk. : alk. paper)
   1. Electricity—Juvenile literature. 2. Electric power—Juvenile literature. [1. Electricity. 2. Electric power.] I. Title. II. Series.
QC527 .2.W93 2003
537—dc21
2002013064

Contents

Chapter 1

The Power of Nature

Electricity is a form of energy. It is caused by the movement of tiny particles called **electrons**. We cannot see electricity, smell it, or hear it, but we know it by what it does. Electricity provides energy for lighting, heating, air conditioning, and cooking. It also powers our televisions and computers.

Electricity can be made, or generated, in power plants. It is then sent over wires to homes and businesses, where it powers the many machines of modern life.

Lightning

The effects of electricity can also be seen in nature. Lightning is caused by the discharge of electrical energy in clouds. The amount of energy discharged is so great that it creates a trail of heat and light. This trail of bright flashes is what people see as lightning bolts. The sound produced by this discharge is called thunder.

There are two common types of lightning. One is called cloud-to-cloud lightning. This type of lightning travels between clouds without ever reaching the ground. The other type is cloud-to-ground lightning. It strikes the earth and objects on it.

Most of the time lightning is just a brilliant show of light. But lightning can do a great deal of damage. When lightning hits a tree, for instance, it might split the trunk all the way to the ground and hurl branches and bark a block or more.

This great surge of power can be deadly. Lightning can release electrical energy of up to 100 million volts.

A bolt of lightning reaches toward the ground during a thunderstorm.

This is an extreme burst of heat and energy. Every year in the United States, about 100 people die and 250 are injured from lightning strikes. Some people who have survived lightning strikes describe feeling numb at first, followed by great pain. A victim of a lightning strike might suffer second- or third-degree burns. Articles of clothing, such as sneakers, scorch or melt.

Cloud-to-cloud and cloud-to-ground lightning are common sights. They strike in locations around the world about one hundred times per second. But other forms of lightninglike electricity also exist. These are rarely seen. Two of the most curious forms are St. Elmo's fire and **ball lightning**.

Unusual Energy

Accounts of St. Elmo's fire date to about the year 300. Sailors noticed that the top of a boat's mast glowed during storms. They thought this was a sign from St. Elmo, the patron saint of early Mediterranean sailors. Since it usually appeared at the end of severe thunderstorms, the sailors saw the glowing mast as a sign that St. Elmo was protecting them from harm. St. Elmo's fire is actually a type of electrical discharge called **corona**. Corona can occur on pointed objects, such as a ship's mast or the pointed spires on the tops of buildings, and has even been observed glowing on the horns of cattle. It is caused by the highly charged atmosphere created by electrical storms.

An artist's depiction shows ball lightning emerging from a dark thundercloud.

Another strange type of lightning, ball lightning, is mentioned in records dating to ancient Greece. Ball lightning is described as a shining sphere, roughly the size of a child's head. It may last from a few seconds to several minutes. It is seen during periods of thundery weather and might appear before, during, or shortly after a thunderstorm.

How Cloud-to-Ground Lightning Occurs

Millions of microscopic particles in the cloud collide and separate creating a charged cloud. Negatively charged particles gather at the bottom of the cloud to produce an electric field.

As the electric field gets more powerful it attracts a positive charge on the ground. The air beneath the cloud breaks down in a process called ionization.

+	Positively charged particles	⬤	Electric field
−	Negatively charged particles	▮▮	Leader
		⬜	Lightning

③

④

The ionized air creates an invisible channel called a leader. The leader reaches toward the positively charged ground below.

Lightning results when the leader reaches Earth, creating a conductive path between the cloud and the ground.

Ball lightning has even been known to occur indoors. One account comes from rural Mississippi during the 1920s. According to this account, a thunderstorm was brewing on a warm summer evening. The family had opened the front and back doors of the house, hoping to catch a cool breeze. Suddenly, what appeared to be a small ball of fire bounced through the front doorway, narrowly missing the family's youngest daughter. It passed through the house and bounced out the back door. The mother later said that, although the frightening incident seemed much longer, the entire episode lasted just over a minute.

Lightning is not the only type of electricity produced by nature. Some of the most interesting and unusual examples of electricity are found in living creatures.

Electrified Fish

Several types of fish actually produce electricity. One of these fish is the electric eel.

The electric eel is not a true eel. It is a type of freshwater fish found in the Amazon River as well as other rivers in South America. It can produce a powerful electric charge.

The eel's electric organ is in its tail, which makes up about 80 percent of the eel's body. Like a battery, the eel's body has two opposite poles—the head and the tail—and it can discharge voltage from either end.

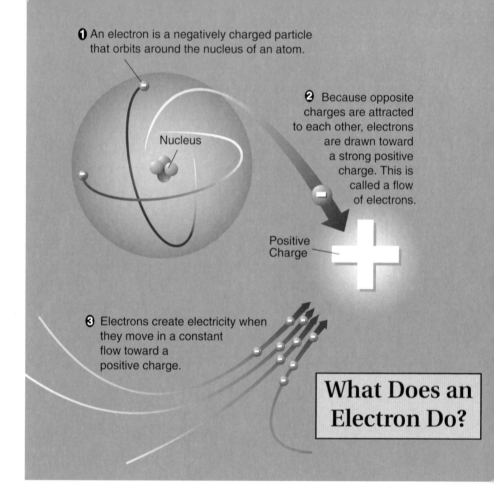

① An electron is a negatively charged particle that orbits around the nucleus of an atom.

Nucleus

② Because opposite charges are attracted to each other, electrons are drawn toward a strong positive charge. This is called a flow of electrons.

Positive Charge

③ Electrons create electricity when they move in a constant flow toward a positive charge.

What Does an Electron Do?

Direct contact with an electric eel can injure or kill humans and large animals. Small eels, those one to two feet long, can produce charges of up to 100 volts. This is enough to cause serious injury to a person. Large eels, five to seven feet long, can produce charges of up to 650 volts of electricity. This is about five times the voltage of a household electrical socket. Because water conducts electricity, this amount of energy can be conducted twenty feet through water to stun an animal as large as a horse.

The eel's electric charge has several purposes. One is to help it catch and eat its prey. The electric eel has no teeth with which to grasp its prey. So it stuns prey with an electric charge. The unmoving prey then poses little challenge for the hungry eel.

The eel also uses its electrical charge for protection. It has no spines, and could be easily attacked and eaten by large animals. The electric field around the eel keeps other animals at a distance.

The electrical charge is also used for navigation. Sometimes waterways inhabited by the electric eel are muddy and murky and its eyes are of little use.

The smallmouth electric catfish uses electric pulses to scavenge for food and ward off predators.

The eel sends out electrical pulses that bounce off of objects and animals, signaling the eel that something is in its way. Some scientists believe that the electric eels also use these low-power pulses to communicate with other eels.

Other fish that rely on electrical charges for navigation include the elephant-nosed fish of South America and the electric catfish and the electric ray, both found in West Africa. All use electrical pulses to make their way through their watery habitats. They also rely on these pulses to find food and fend off predators.

The sight of bolts of lightning cracking across the sky and stories of fish that can stun a person with an electric charge have prompted a great deal of curiosity over the years. The study of these natural forms of electricity began long ago. Gaining an understanding of electricity and how it can be used has continued for many centuries.

Chapter 2

Pioneers in Electricity and Magnetism

In ancient times, people observed two unusual forces that caused objects to move mysteriously by themselves. One of these forces was later named static electricity. Static electricity causes some objects to be attracted to each other. The other force came to be called magnetism. Magnetism causes certain metals to be attracted to lodestone, a magnetic iron ore.

Although these two forces are connected, the earliest discoveries did not show that connection. The earliest discoveries revealed only that these forces exist. Curiosity then prompted people to seek more information about electricity and magnetism.

Earliest Experimenters

During the sixth century B.C., a Greek mathematician named Thales made an odd discovery. He was holding a piece of **amber** in his hand when his cat rubbed against his legs. He bent over pet to the cat with the amber still in his hand and noticed that the cat's fur stood on end. The amber appeared to have the power of attraction. Today scientists know that rubbing the amber created a static electric charge that attracted the cat's fur.

Magnetism was also discovered by accident. During the fourth century B.C., Chinese emperor Huang-Li found that when a polished lodestone was placed on a highly polished block of wood, the lodestone always pointed north. This discovery led to the development of the compass.

The ancient Greek mathematician Thales (above) discovered that amber has a static electric charge. At right, a piece of amber attracts a feather.

Interest Spreads

Interest in these two natural forces grew. Scientists conducted experiments to learn more about both forces. Little by little they found that experimenting with magnets was fairly easy because magnets have a steady pull. Experimenting with static electricity was more difficult because static electricity occurs only in short bursts. To learn more about electrical energy, scientists needed a way of producing a constant flow of electricity.

German physicist Otto von Guericke built such a machine in the 1600s. He put sulfur in a glass globe and mounted the globe on a crank-turned shaft. When he cranked the shaft, it rotated the globe. To cause friction, he held a cloth to the globe as it rotated. Sparks created by the friction then jumped to brushes touching the globe. Guericke's **generator** was a novelty.

Later, experimenters attached wires to generators such as the one built by von Guericke. They learned that electrical energy could flow through the wires. This led some experimenters to believe that electricity was a type of invisible liquid. If electricity was a liquid, scientists reasoned, maybe it could be collected and stored in a bottle like other liquid. In 1745 E.G. von Kleist of Germany created a device that could store electricity. This storage device was called a **Leyden jar**. It was named for the University of Leyden in the Netherlands, where many experi-

Otto von Guericke approaches his generator in this undated drawing.

ments with electricity were being conducted. Von Kleist ran a wire through a cork and into a bottle of water. He then used the generator to charge the water. When he disconnected and removed the generator and touched the wire, he received a powerful shock. From this, von Kleist and other experimenters learned that electricity could be stored for later use. If several Leyden jars were attached to a machine that made static electricity, experimenters could create fire and melt wires.

While testing the electrical charge created in the Leyden jars, scientists observed sparks resembling tiny lightning bolts. They wondered if there was a connection between these sparks and lightning. This question would be answered by Benjamin Franklin.

Understanding Electricity

Benjamin Franklin lived in the English colonies in America. He attended a demonstration of electricity in Boston in 1746 and was so impressed by the demonstration that he bought his own equipment and set up a laboratory. He knew that scientists had been experimenting with electricity for many years but had not been able to explain how and why electricity moves.

One of the first things Franklin noticed in his own experiments was that some substances seemed to gain electric fluid while others seemed to lose it. Glass, for example, seemed to gain electric fluid after being rubbed while amber seemed to lose electric fluid. From this, he concluded that there were not two types of electrical fluids, as some earlier experimenters believed. Instead, Franklin suggested, there existed one kind of electrical fluid and two kinds of charges. He called the gain in electrical fluid a positive charge and the loss a negative charge.

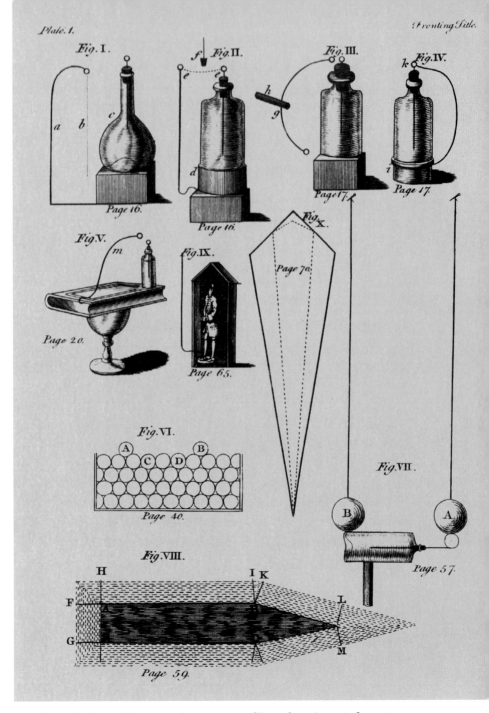

Benjamin Franklin used a series of Leyden jars (above) to show that electricity was composed of positive and negative charges.

The Lightning Rod

As Franklin continued with his experiments, he discovered that a metal rod conducts electricity. This means it allows electricity to flow through it. Franklin wondered if he could use a metal rod to attract electricity from the atmosphere. He believed that if the rod could attract electricity, it should also attract lightning. So, in 1752 he made a device he called a lightning rod. Franklin set up his lightning rod in a high place on his own house. One end pointed to the sky. The other end was connected to the ground.

He attached bells to his lightning rod. He would know when the rod was electrified because the charge would cause the bells to ring. Franklin found that lightning behaved a lot like the static electricity created in earlier experiments. From this he concluded that lightning was a form of electricity.

But Franklin was not satisfied just attracting lightning through a rod. He also experimented with flying kites in thunderstorms to attract electricity. The charge flowed down the long wet cord to a key at the bottom of the cord. Sparks jumped from the key to his fingers when he moved his hand close to the key. He had discovered another way to conduct electricity.

Franklin put some of his experiments to practical use. Many homes and businesses at this time were built of wood, and lightning strikes from thunderstorms often caused fires. Franklin realized that a rod attached to a building and connected to the ground could protect that building from a lightning strike. As in his experiments, lightning would be attracted to the metal rod rather than the building. The rod would conduct the force of the lightning strike toward the ground. This would leave the building undamaged. And this is exactly how they

Franklin uses a kite and a key to show that electricity will flow through a wet kite string.

worked. Franklin sold his lightning rods to the public, and many homes and businesses were saved from lightning strikes.

Aside from his lightning rods, Franklin had proved through his experiments that lightning (or electricity) could be controlled. This new knowledge would lead to the development of many practical uses for electricity.

Chapter 3

Controlling the Power

Benjamin Franklin had discovered ways of attracting and conducting electricity. Interest now shifted to figuring out how to use it. The brief bursts of electrical power known as static electricity were not a reliable source of energy. To be useful, electrical power would have to flow in a constant, steady stream. This flow of electricity came to be called a **current**.

The ability to conduct a current of electricity would lead to the invention of new forms of communication and transportation, and new methods of manufacturing. Several people were responsible for the ideas and devices that ultimately led to putting electricity to practical use.

Alessandro Volta

In the early 1790s, Italian physicist Alessandro Volta discovered that he could use two different types of metals to produce an electric current. This discovery came about while Volta's friend Luigi Giovani was

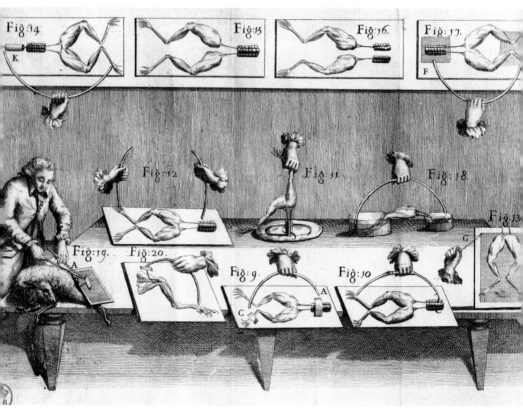

In this illustration Italian physicist Alessandro Volta uses frog legs to conduct electric experiments.

dissecting a frog. Suddenly, in the middle of the procedure, the frog's leg began twitching. Giovani thought the twitching might have been caused by lightning. Volta was not sure. He repeated the procedure to see if he could find the cause. This time, though, it was a clear day. Again the muscle twitched. After several years of experimenting, Volta concluded that weather had not been responsible for the twitching. Rather, the two different metal plates holding the wet muscle tissue had produced an electric charge. The charge had caused the frog's muscle to twitch.

Volta used the results of his experiments to make the first wet battery, called the voltaic pile. It was made from disks of copper and zinc separated by disks of heavy paper soaked in salt water or acid, both of which are excellent **conductors**. Copper wire was attached to the top and the bottom of the pile of disks. When Volta connected the wires to close the circuit, a continuous flow of electrical energy resulted.

Volta had invented a device that produced a steadily flowing current, or an electrical circuit. His invention provided a source of power for many future experiments and the development of many useful electrical devices.

Hans Christian Oersted

Even more exciting advances were on the way thanks to the work of Hans Christian Oersted. Oersted was a professor of science at Copenhagen University in Denmark in 1820. Although it was not the accepted belief among scientists of the time, Oersted thought there was a relationship between electricity and magnetism.

In 1820 Oersted invited his students to a demonstration of how electric current could heat a wire. A compass happened to be nearby. When Oersted turned on the electric current, the compass needle moved. In fact, every time he switched on the current, the needle pointed at the electrically charged wire.

Oersted realized that the moving electric current must be generating a magnetic field. And the magnetic field had moved the compass needle. This

In this 1820 illustration Hans Christian Oersted shows how an electric current moves a compass needle.

The magnetic force that holds these magnetite particles together is similar to the force generated in Oersted's experiment.

meant that electricity could somehow produce magnetism. Ten years later, another scientist would take Oersted's discovery a step farther.

Michael Faraday

British scientist Michael Faraday read about Oersted's discovery that electricity could produce magnetism. If that was so, Faraday thought, it should also be possible for magnetism to create electricity. His idea seemed reasonable, but he and other scientists experimented many months with magnets and metal wires without producing an electric current. Finally, Faraday used a moving magnet, and in 1831 he proved that a turning magnet would produce an electric current.

This and other discoveries showed scientists the link between electricity and magnetism. Later scientists came to understand that electricity and magnetism are part of one force, called electromagnetic force. Faraday's work put electricity on a practical path. His experiment with the turning magnet led to a means of creating and supplying large amounts of electricity.

Putting Electricity to Work

Thanks to Faraday's discoveries, later inventors and scientists created many useful devices. In the late nineteenth century, for example, electric motors began powering machines once driven by steam. The electric motor dramatically sped up production of factory items such as textiles. And between 1802 and 1809 a crude form of electric light, called an arc lamp, replaced gas lamps. Arc lamps were lit by means of a continuous electric spark between carbon rods. The lights were bright. They allowed factories to operate into the night. But they were also inefficient and needed constant maintenance.

A reliable form of electric lighting was not far off, however. American inventor Thomas Edison spent

Thomas Edison uses a wood-burning stove and carbonized paper during one of his many experiments with electric lighting.

Thomas Edison (center) illuminates the first long-lasting lightbulb in 1879.

hundreds of hours experimenting with different ways of providing a steady glow of light over a long period.

Edison finally developed the first long-lasting lightbulb in 1879. He and his assistants watched it, around the clock, as it glowed steadily for forty hours. The bulb lit when an electric current caused the carbon filament, a thin wire in an oxygen-free glass bulb, to heat white-hot. This produced a bright glow. They had succeeded beyond anyone's hopes.

Within three years the world's first electric power plant had opened in New York City. The Pearl Street Power Plant was a symbol of a new era. A single power plant could generate electricity around the clock and send that electricity to homes and businesses nearby. As more power plants were built, more homes and businesses could benefit from this new technology. Life no longer had to revolve around day and night. A constant source of electricity allowed businesses to run all day and through the night. Activities in the home could also continue well after dark. Many new labor-saving devices soon followed. Thanks to the work of dozens of scientists and inventors, the modern era was about to begin.

Chapter 4

Evolving Technology

As the nineteenth century came to close, inventors began experimenting with many different ways of using electricity. Telephones, televisions, computers, and high-speed trains are just a few of the advances that grew out of these experiments.

Communication

Electric currents had already made rapid communication possible by means of the telegraph. The next step in communication was the telephone. The telephone, invented by Alexander Graham Bell, used a thin membrane to re-create the vibrations of the human voice. Electric current carried those vibrations from sender to receiver. By boosting the current, Bell ensured that the sender's voice reached the person on the other end.

The telephone was an important new form of communication but not the only one. Record players and radios also relied on electricity to send or enhance sound.

Motion pictures used electricity to project pictures on a big screen.

Television was yet another advancement in communication. In 1927 Philo Farnsworth built a device that could transmit an electronic image directly into people's homes. This device became known as the television.

Later in the twentieth century inventors came up with the most advanced form of communication yet. The electronic superhighway is a global system

Engineers operate electronic display panels used to monitor global telephone systems.

of electronic communication made possible by computers. Without electricity there would be no computers.

The earliest computers were huge room-size units. They held thousands of vacuum tubes. Each tube represented one number or one small bit of information, such as a letter or a symbol. The vacuum tubes acted as switches, conveying information by turning electric currents off and on.

The thousands of vacuum tubes inside the computers had to heat up before they would perform their functions. One large computer in Philadelphia called ENIAC needed 150,000 watts of electricity every day to operate.

Computers became smaller and more efficient over time, as first transistors and then small silicon wafers, called chips, replaced the vacuum tubes. These chips became smaller and smaller and were called microchips. Today's tiny silicon chips can store millions of bits of information.

Computer technology is changing every day. Maybe the one constant piece of this technology is the electrical energy that powers this important form of communication.

Transportation

Electrical energy also brought about many changes in transportation. Before electrically powered motors and current electricity, people depended on

Computers like the huge ENIAC (pictured) have been replaced by computers that use tiny silicon microchips (inset) to store information.

horses and steam-powered trains. One of the first ways electricity improved transportation was by enabling many people to move around towns.

The first-known electric trolley car operated in Wisconsin in 1886. Trolley cars grew in popularity

How Much Electricity Do These Appliances Use in an Hour?

Light Bulb
75 Watts

CD Player
50 Watts

Color TV
300 Watts

Laptop
Computer
20 Watts

Blender
350 Watts

until over eight thousand miles of trolley tracks were in use between 1925 and 1933. Trolleys were the size of small buses. Tracks ran up the center of a street with lines for the electric current running overhead. A rod with a grooved metal wheel on top ran from the electric wire to the trolley's roof. The grooved metal wheel conducted electricity through the rod and down a wire to the car's gearbox, which turned the wheels.

High-Speed Trains

Trolleys lost their appeal with the invention of affordable automobiles. The most popular cars had gasoline-fueled engines, but batteries were needed to provide the spark to start the engines. Even today, automobiles need batteries to operate.

Different ways of getting around are still being improved and refined. Electricity is responsible for some of these changes.

Electric high-speed trains operate all over the world. Bullet trains, as they are sometimes called, can be seen zipping through Japan at 125 miles per hour. France and Great Britain also have high-speed trains. On some routes, the French trains reach speeds of up to 186 miles per hour. In western Europe, thousands of miles of track are being upgraded to support a network of high-speed electric trains that will connect major cities. Some of these trains will travel at speeds up to 200 miles per hour.

High-speed electric trains of the future may be able to go more than three hundred miles per hour. This new generation of trains is called the maglev train. Maglev is short for magnetic levitation. The maglev train runs with the help of superconducting magnets. These magnets lift the train above the

This elevated train in Sydney, Australia runs on electricity and connects the city's many neighborhoods.

track and also propel it forward. This idea is yet another advancement in the ways of using electricity and magnetism.

Making and Moving Electric Energy

As needs for electricity grow, more ways of generating electrical power have been developed. Electricity is made by using heat sources such as natural gas, oil, coal, and nuclear and solar power. Electric power plants, which supply electricity to cities and towns, convert mechanical energy to electrical energy. To do this, the station uses an engine, or **turbine**, and a water wheel or some other device to drive the generator.

Most of the electricity used in the United States is produced in steam turbines. Steam turbines have blades mounted on a shaft. Steam is forced against the blades, rotating the shaft. The shaft is connected to the generator, which converts the mechanical energy from the turbine into electrical energy. In the generator, a coil of wire spins within a magnetic field. Each section of the coil is a separate electric conductor, which moves a current of electricity. All of the currents together make up one large current. This current travels along wires into homes and businesses to supply electrical energy.

Over half of the electricity in the United States is created by fossil fuels such as oil and gas. A little

Solar cells like these absorb energy from the sun and store it in batteries to be used at a later time.

more than 20 percent comes from nuclear power plants. Nuclear power plants use a process called fission to create electricity. This process splits the nuclei of atoms of uranium, releasing heat energy, which makes steam to turn turbines. But nuclear fission creates radioactive waste, which can be very dangerous. Nuclear fusion is a much safer process that does not create harmful waste. Although nuclear fusion is an expensive process today, people continue to find ways to make this safer type of nuclear energy more affordable.

Renewable Power

Renewable power sources are used in much smaller percentages. They are solar, hydropower (water-driven), geothermal (heat produced deep within the earth), and wind power.

The sun is the most readily available renewable resource. Solar cells, called **photovoltaics**, are installed on roofs or other areas that receive direct light from the sun. They gather solar energy that can be directly converted into electrical energy. The electrical energy is stored in batteries until needed. Solar cells do not need power stations or fossil fuels to create electricity.

Scientists are always looking at new ways to fuel power plants. Possibilities include the use of decaying plant matter. As plant matter ferments, it makes alcohol. Alcohol can be burned to produce heat for the turbines.

Scientists have not yet explored all of the possible ways to produce and use electricity. As long as there are people with imagination willing to push the limits and think beyond currently accepted ideas, there will be more discoveries of new uses for this awesome power.

Glossary

amber: A translucent fossil that developed from tree sap; color may range from pale yellow to reddish brown.

ball lightning: A rare form of lightning made up of luminous balls of electrical energy; it may move across solid surfaces or float in the air.

conductor: A material or object that allows the flow of an electric current.

corona: A glow surrounding an electrically conductive material.

current: A flow of electrical energy.

electron: A negatively charged particle of an atom.

generator: A device that changes mechanical energy into electrical energy.

Leyden jar: The first device created that would briefly store electrical energy.

photovoltaic: Material that takes in solar energy to be converted into electrical energy.

turbine: A series of curved blades attached to a rotating shaft; steam, air, or water causes the blades to turn.

For Further Exploration

Charles K. Adams, *Nature's Electricity*. Blue Ridge Summit, PA: Tab Books, 1987. This book provides illustrated examples of forms of electricity found in nature.

Robert Gardner, *Electricity and Magnetism*. New York: Twenty-First Century Books, 1994. The author narrates the earliest experiments in electricity; it also provides activities for students as well as color illustrations.

Martin J. Gutnik, *Electricity: From Faraday to Solar Generators*. New York: Franklin Watts, 1986. Black-and-white photographs and diagrams illustrate the science of electromagnetism from Faraday, through electronic communication, and to the electric light-bulb.

Irwin Math, *Wires and Watts: Understanding Electricity*. New York: Charles Schribner's Sons, 1981. This book offers a brief history with dia-grammed experiments, including the units of measurement associated with electricity.

Larry E. Schafer, *Taking Charge: An Introduction to Electricity*. Washington, DC: National Science Teachers Association, 1992. The historical background of electricity is linked to a wide variety of activities for students.

Sheila Wyborny, *Thomas Edison*. San Diego: Kid-Haven, 2002. This book details the life and achievements of Thomas Edison, inventor of the lightbulb and motion pictures, and holder over a thousand patents during his lifetime.

Index

acid, 25
amber, 14–15, 18
arc lamps, 28
automobiles, 37

ball lightning, 6, 7, 10
batteries, 23–25, 37
Bell, Alexander Graham, 32
bullet trains, 37

cars, 37
charge types, 18
chips, computer, 34
cloud-to-cloud lightning, 4–5, 6
cloud-to-ground lightning, 5, 6
communications, 32–34
compasses, 15
computers, 34
conductor(s)
  acid as, 25
  experiments with, 18, 20–22
  metal (lightning) rods as, 20–22
  water as, 11, 25
coronas, 6
current
  described, 23
  first battery and, 23–25
  light bulbs and, 28, 30–31
  produced by magnetism, 27–28

Edison, Thomas, 28, 30–31

electric catfish, 13
electric eels, 10–13
electric lights, 28, 30–31
electric motors, 28
electric rays, 13
electrified fish, 10–13
electromagnetic force, 28
electrons, 4
elephant-nosed fish, 13
ENIAC (computer), 34
Europe, 37
experiments
  with conductors, 18, 20–22
  with current, 23–25, 27–28, 30–31
  with generators, 16
  with lightning, 20–22
  with magnetic fields, 16, 25–28
  with static electricity, 16
  with storage devices, 16–18

Faraday, Michael, 27–28
Farnsworth, Philo, 33
fish, 10–13
fission, 40
fossil fuels, 39
France, 37
Franklin, Benjamin, 18, 20–22
fusion, 40

generators
  first, 16
  power plants, 31, 39–41
geothermal power, 41

Picture Credits

Cover: © Henry Dakin/Science Photo Library

© Archivo Iconografico, S.A./CORBIS, 24

© Associated Press/The Holland Sentinal, 27

© AT&T/Blackbirch Press, 33

© The Bakken Library and Museum, 15 (bottom), 17

© Julian Baum/Science Photo Library, 7

© Bettmann/CORBIS, 21, 35

© J-L Charmet/Science Photo Library, 15 (top)

Digital Stock, Inc., 38

© Mary Evans Picture Library, 26

Chris Jouan, 8-9, 11

Library of Congress, 19, 29

NOAA, 5

Brandy Noon, 36

© OSF/Gibbs, M./AnimalsAnimals, 12

PhotoDisc, 35 (inset), 40

© Schenectady Museum; Hall of Electrical History
Foundation/CORBIS

Sheila Wyborny is a retired science and social studies teacher. She lives in Houston, Texas, with her husband, Wendell, a broadcast engineer. The Wybornys enjoy flying their own aircraft, collecting antiques, and spending time with family and friends.